Today God
Wants You To
Know. . .

*You Are
Loved*

Today God
Wants You To
Know. . .
You Are
Loved

Laura
Wegener

BARBOUR BOOKS
An Imprint of Barbour Publishing, Inc.

ISBN 978-1-64352-154-1

Scripture quotations marked KJV are taken from the King James Version of the Bible.

Scripture quotations marked ESV are from The Holy Bible, English Standard Version®, copyright © 2001 by Crossway Bibles, a publishing ministry of Good News Publishers. Used by permission. All rights reserved.

Scripture quotations marked NLT are taken from the Holy Bible, New Living Translation copyright© 1996, 2004, 2015 by Tyndale House Foundation. Used by permission of Tyndale House Publishers, Inc. Carol Stream, Illinois 60188. All rights reserved.

Scripture quotations marked AMP are taken from the Amplified® Bible, © 1954, 1958, 1962, 1964, 1965, 1987 by The Lockman Foundation. Used by permission.

Scripture quotations marked MSG are from THE MESSAGE. Copyright © by Eugene H. Peterson 1993, 1994, 1995, 1996, 2000, 2001, 2002. Used by permission of NavPress Publishing Group.

Scripture quotations marked NIV are taken from the HOLY BIBLE, NEW INTERNATIONAL VERSION®. NIV®. Copyright © 1973, 1978, 1984, 2011 by Biblica, Inc.™ Used by permission. All rights reserved worldwide.

Published by Barbour Books, an imprint of Barbour Publishing, Inc., 1810 Barbour Drive, Uhrichsville, Ohio 44683, www.barbourbooks.com

Our mission is to inspire the world with the life-changing message of the Bible.

Member of the
Evangelical Christian
Publishers Association

Printed in the United States of America.

Contents

Introduction

God loves you. He cares about you deeply and is interested in your daily life. Everything about you brings a smile to His face. Isn't that amazing?

Because God loves you, you can love Him back. What does that look like? That's what this book is about. It's a glimpse of how we can live our lives in response to His love.

So let's learn together what God's promises are to us—what He enables us to do!—as we begin to understand "how wide, how long, how high, and how deep his love is [for us]" (Ephesians 3:18 NLT).

CONFIDENCE

You Are Chosen

You are a chosen race, a royal priesthood, a holy nation, a people for his own possession, that you may proclaim the excellencies of him who called you out of darkness into his marvelous light.

1 Peter 2:9 esv

My mom and I used to hunt for Nancy Drew books at antique stores. When I found a book I was hunting for, it was a thrill. I knew that chosen piece was special to me and unlike the rest.

In the same way, you've been handpicked for God's family. You are special to Him!

You Are Beautiful

*Don't be concerned about the outward beauty
of fancy hairstyles, expensive jewelry, or beautiful
clothes. You should clothe yourselves instead with
the beauty that comes from within, the unfading
beauty of a gentle and quiet spirit,
which is so precious to God.*
1 PETER 3:3–4 NLT

Something blossoms in women when we get our
hair done and put on a fancy dress. We love to
look beautiful.

The greatest beauty, though, doesn't come
with extra mascara or hairspray. It comes from
within. Wear your smile, and love the Lord;
you'll shine from the inside out.

You Are Unique

*"Before I formed you in the womb I knew you,
and before you were born I consecrated you;
I appointed you a prophet to the nations."*

Jeremiah 1:5 esv

No one else in the world is just like you. Your hair, your eyes, your looks. Your personality, your smile, your charm. Absolutely everything about you is special. God created you to be exactly who you are.

When self-doubt surfaces, think about what makes you special. Know that God has made you as He did for a reason. You can embrace your beauty.

You Are at Peace

*Therefore, since we have been justified
by faith, we have peace with God
through our Lord Jesus Christ.*

ROMANS 5:1 ESV

Whether you're a soccer mom transporting kids everywhere, a businesswoman, a student juggling classes, or a combination of all three, peace may seem like the last thing possible to achieve. Yet, the myriad of activities in your life do not need to upset your inner peace. Nothing you do—or don't do—will ever take away your standing of righteousness with God. Live with confidence that you have been made righteous in Him!

You Are God's Friend

*"I'm no longer calling you servants because servants
don't understand what their master is thinking and
planning. No, I've named you friends because I've
let you in on everything I've heard from the Father."*
JOHN 15:15 MSG

My best friend and I have known each other
for over two decades. We know each other's
strengths, faults, and weaknesses—and we still
love to spend time together.

God considers you His friend. He knows everything about you, including your flaws, yet He still
loves you deeply. He wants to spend time with
you!

You Are Able

"Get out of here, Satan," Jesus told him. "For the Scriptures say, 'You must worship the Lord your God and serve only him.' " Then the devil went away.

MATTHEW 4:10–11 NLT

I can't comprehend the thoughts running through Jesus' head on the fortieth day of His fast. He was ravenous and beyond exhausted, yet He still had the ability to say no to the enemy, three times in a row.

If Jesus could do it then, we can do it now. We can say no to the enemy. We are able because He first did.

You Are Not Alone

For God has said, "I will never fail you.
I will never abandon you."

Hebrews 13:5 NLT

The older I get, the more I come across situations I have no idea how to handle. I think, *I just want someone to tell me what to do!*

One day, the Lord brought me to Hebrews 13:5, and I was reminded that God is with us through every situation we face. If we need help or direction, we can trust that Voice on the inside to provide us with the right way to go.

You Are Influential

*Death and life are in the power of
the tongue: and they that love it
shall eat the fruit thereof.*

PROVERBS 18:21 KJV

The direction of my life was deeply impacted by
my tenth-grade teacher's verbal encouragement—
words she probably doesn't remember speaking
at all. It's the perfect reminder that our influence
extends far greater than we realize, and much of
that influence starts in our mouth. Our words have
great impact. Use this influence wisely.

You Are Cared For

*"And which of you by being anxious can add a
single hour to his span of life? . . .
But if God so clothes the grass of the field,
which today is alive and tomorrow
is thrown into the oven, will he not
much more clothe you?"*

MATTHEW 6:27, 30 ESV

Worry can feel productive; it's as though thinking and rethinking through the situation will change it. The truth, though, is worry only changes your stress level.

God cares for you and knows the situation you are facing. Rest in Him; He'll take care of you.

You Are Part of Something Big

*The suffering won't last forever. It won't be long
before this generous God who has great plans for us
in Christ—eternal and glorious plans they are!—will
have you put together and on your feet for good.
He gets the last word; yes, he does.*

1 PETER 5:10–11 MSG

No circumstance or person will ever be strong
enough to push our God out of the way. Even
His haters will ultimately bow their knee before
His throne. So when the going gets tough, always
remember that, in the end, God wins.

PRAYER

You Can Bring Heaven to Earth

"May your Kingdom come soon. May your will be done on earth, as it is in heaven."

Matthew 6:10 NLT

God wants you to be a part of His work on earth. He longs for you to exercise your faith in His will. This is because God has included us in His plans through our prayers. Our prayers enable us to access God in heaven. What a privilege!

If you want something from heaven to come to earth, pray. Entreat God to make it happen.

You Can Come Boldly

So let us come boldly
to the throne of our gracious God.

HEBREWS 4:16 NLT

When I was younger, I was greatly impacted by Brother Jesse Duplantis's morning routine. He'd wake and say, "Hello, God." He'd hear, "Hi, Jesse!"

My thoughts raced. God doesn't play favorites. If he can be that close to God, I can too. So that's what I do—I approach God boldly. He is my Lord, and He's also my friend.

He loves you as He loves me and Jesse. Take down religious barriers, and talk to Him as a friend.

You Can Rest

Be still before the L<small>ORD</small> and wait patiently
for him; fret not yourself over the one
who prospers in his way, over the man
who carries out evil devices!
P<small>SALM</small> 37:7 <small>ESV</small>

Waiting for prayers to be answered is quite the
test of patience. Usually, we want our prayers
answered—now! But God doesn't work like that.
He sees the big picture of our lives as well as
the lives of everyone else in the world. Our job
is to bring Him our prayers and cares, and then
trust Him to answer.

You Can Intercede

*"I searched for someone to stand in the gap
in the wall so I wouldn't have to destroy
the land, but I found no one."*

Ezekiel 22:30 NLT

Millions across this world need God. If you know Him, you can pray for God to reach them with His love. Now, you can't pray for everyone by name, but you can pray for other people as you are led. Random thoughts about friends, acquaintances, even celebrities, can be turned into prayers of intercession for their salvation. God desires for you to pray so He can impact their lives.

You Can Be Patient

*Follow the example of those who are going
to inherit God's promises because
of their faith and endurance.*
HEBREWS 6:12 NLT

Because God loves you, you don't have to be concerned about when you will see your prayers answered. All you have to do is trust that they will be answered.

In many situations we bring to the Lord, multiple unknowns are in play—including the feelings and prayers of other people. God is the only one who sees everything, so He orchestrates life in a way that only He can. Trust Him to do so.

You Can Intercede for Your Nation

"Make yourselves at home there and work for the country's welfare. Pray for Babylon's well-being. If things go well for Babylon, things will go well for you."

JEREMIAH 29:7 MSG

I'm learning how to include prayers for America in my daily living. Sometimes it's just by sending up "flare prayers"—that's what my middle school teacher called those quick prayers you utter as you think of someone. Other times, it's good to sit and pray more specific lengthy prayers. Either way, keep your country in your prayers. When it prospers, you prosper.

You Can Ask for Understanding

*[That] the eyes of your understanding being
enlightened; that ye may know what is the hope
of his calling, and what the riches of the
glory of his inheritance in the saints.*

EPHESIANS 1:18 KJV

Every day we are presented with new opportunities and unique decisions where we don't know what to do. In these situations, pray what Paul prayed: "God, please open my understanding to Your will." Trust that He will show you exactly what you need to know—and if the situation involves others, you can pray for them too!

You Can Give God Time

Then he added, "Pay close attention to what you hear. The closer you listen, the more understanding you will be given—and you will receive even more."
MARK 4:24 NLT

Have you ever started a conversation with someone who walked away halfway through your first sentence? It's as though they didn't hear you talk. Maybe they started the conversation but left before listening? Do you think God feels like that sometimes?

Do more than just quickly read the Bible or blurt out your prayer requests. Spend time with God. He wants to talk to you!

You Can Tune
Your Heart to God

*"But the Helper, the Holy Spirit, whom the Father
will send in my name, he will teach you all things
and bring to your remembrance all
that I have said to you."*

JOHN 14:26 ESV

The Holy Spirit is constantly talking to you, prompting you to remember the Bible in different situations you face. He even helps you in your daily tasks. The urge to make sure you didn't leave your wallet on the kitchen counter? That's often Him! The more you recognize Him, the more you hear Him and learn to respond.

You Can Turn
Your Thoughts into Prayer

Pray without ceasing.
1 Thessalonians 5:17 KJV

Whether it's natural disasters, a horrible crime, or a celebrity's recent struggles, the media is always telling us what's happening in this world—and a lot of times it isn't good. When I find myself dwelling too long on what is happening, I am learning to turn my thoughts into prayers. I can pray for people whom I will never meet, and I believe God will hear my prayers and impact their lives in some way.

You Can Move Mountains

Elijah was as human as we are, and yet when he prayed earnestly that no rain would fall, none fell for three and a half years! Then, when he prayed again, the sky sent down rain and the earth began to yield its crops.

JAMES 5:17–18 NLT

Our prayers are backed up by the power of this world's Creator. When we pray in faith, anything can happen. Elijah had direction from God to pray for rain; we have the Word of God. Pray the Word, and watch it come to life!

You Can Pray for Others

*And the LORD restored the fortunes of Job, when he
had prayed for his friends. And the LORD gave
Job twice as much as he had before.*

JOB 42:10 ESV

When going through a difficult time, it's easy
to live inward. Everything we pray, say, and do
is focused on our needs. The interesting thing,
though, is that Job—who had every right to be
focused on his difficulties—saw his life changed
when he turned his life outward and prayed for
others. Let that teach us to do the same.

You Can Be Persistent

[Elijah] cast himself down upon the earth, and put his face between his knees, and said to his servant, Go up now, look toward the sea. And he went up, and looked, and said, There is nothing. And he said, Go again seven times. And it came to pass at the seventh time, that he said, Behold, there ariseth a little cloud out of the sea, like a man's hand.
1 KINGS 18:42–44 KJV

Circumstances change when we are bold enough to be persistent in our prayers. Elijah lived this truth; so can we.

You Can Pray for Yourself

If you need wisdom, ask our
generous God, and he will give it to you.
He will not rebuke you for asking.

JAMES 1:5 NLT

Sometimes when I pray through the Pauline prayers found in Ephesians 1 and 3, Colossians 1, and Philippians 1, I don't include my name. Then one day, when I was stumped on how to respond to someone else, I realized that I needed prayer to know how to handle others.

When you're faced with a sticky situation, pray for the other person—and for yourself!

You Can Pray for Your Family

*That he would grant you, according to the riches of
his glory, to be strengthened with might
by his Spirit in the inner man.*

EPHESIANS 3:16 KJV

The routine of living with someone can unintention-ally cause us to forget that our family needs prayer too. In particular, we should provide the strongest prayer support for our husbands. Even if you're not yet married, start praying for him!

If you don't know what to pray, go to the Bible. There you'll find prayers to pray for family that will encourage you in the process.

You Can Embrace Change

For you know that when your faith is tested,
your endurance has a chance to grow.

JAMES 1:3 NLT

I hate change. The problem is, my husband and I want a new house. In order to make this journey easier, I need to view it as a chance to grow.

My trust in God will increase as we search for the right home. It'll be stretched again as we wait for the buyer who wants to purchase our home. Because this will strengthen my patience and trust in God, I will ask God for help to embrace change.

You Can Enjoy God's Word

All Scripture is inspired by God and is useful to teach
us what is true and to make us realize what is wrong
in our lives. It corrects us when we are wrong
and teaches us to do what is right.

2 Timothy 3:16 nlt

Reading the Bible can be intimidating, but only when you don't understand its purpose. The Bible has the power to do amazing things in us. If you have trouble reading the Word, ask the Holy Spirit to help. He'll make the Bible come alive for you!

You Can Give Thanks

*Always giving thanks to God the Father for all things,
in the name of our Lord Jesus Christ.*

EPHESIANS 5:20 AMP

One of my favorite moments when something good has happened is the moment I remember to say, "Thanks!" to the Lord. In that moment, I am reminded of God's faithfulness. I try to keep that habit going even when bad things happen— because we always have something we can be thankful for.

You Can Ask

"Keep on asking, and you will receive what you ask for. Keep on seeking, and you will find. Keep on knocking, and the door will be opened to you."

MATTHEW 7:7 NLT

With all the emphasis God places on prayer in the Bible, it's funny we sometimes forget to ask God for simple things. We don't need to relegate prayer to "big" things. We also don't need to stop asking because we don't see the answer we want. We can ask God for anything and keep bringing our prayers before Him. He'll answer our prayers!

You Can Agree

"Again I say to you, if two of you agree on earth about anything they ask, it will be done for them by my Father in heaven."

MATTHEW 18:19 ESV

Did you know there is power available in agreement? When you and someone else gather together and pray, you unleash a greater power than when you pray on your own. So the next time someone asks you for prayer, don't wait until you're alone. Access a greater power and agree together with them in prayer then and there!

TRUSTING GOD

You Don't Have to Agree

*And David danced before the LORD with all his might
. . . . So David and all the people of Israel brought
up the Ark of the LORD with shouts of joy.*

2 SAMUEL 6:14–15 NLT

King David had watched Uzzah die when he touched the Ark of the Covenant three months prior to these verses found in 2 Samuel. David had been angry and afraid of God, but he didn't allow either feeling to stay. The draw of the Lord's presence was strong, and David allowed his trust of the Lord to be limitless. That's what he focused on when he praised.

You Don't Have to Know Why

Trust G OD from the bottom of your heart;
don't try to figure out everything on your own.
PROVERBS 3:5 MSG

Recently, I saw a blackout curtain on sale while shopping. *Buy it.* This distinct thought felt God-given, but because I didn't understand why I needed the curtain, I didn't buy it.

Within a day, I realized my kids were waking up early because the sun was too bright in their room. Back to the store I went, remembering again that I don't have to understand what the Holy Spirit tells me. All I have to do is obey.

You Don't Have to Know the Timing

God has made everything beautiful for its own time.
ECCLESIASTES 3:11 NLT

Waiting for your spouse—or for your children or grandchildren—can be a frustrating, slow process. That's why I felt slightly guilty that I got married four years before my best friend even met her spouse. Now I realize that the timing for both of us was perfect. She couldn't have married her honey any sooner, and I couldn't have married my man later. We blossomed in love when we trusted God with His perfect timing.

You Don't Have to Know When

So let's not get tired of doing what is good.
At just the right time we will reap a harvest
of blessing if we don't give up.

GALATIANS 6:9 NLT

I'm one of many moms who has a baby in heaven. Brody Mark came at twenty-one weeks. My arms ached the months following his birthday; I couldn't fathom feeling right again. Now I have my arms full with his two brothers. I didn't know when it would happen, but my day came.

Keep trusting God with your heart. Your day will come too.

You Don't Have to Know the Reason

"My thoughts are nothing like your thoughts,"
says the Lord. "And my ways are far beyond
anything you could imagine."

Isaiah 55:8 nlt

I vividly remember when I had the unusual thought to turn one street earlier than normal on my way to school. I dismissed the thought as silly. When I saw the road I normally turn on was blocked with a police car, I rethought my actions.

God is always directing our steps in simple ways. Our job is to tune out our heads and tune in to our hearts.

You Don't Have to Know How

But my God shall supply all your need according to his riches in glory by Christ Jesus.
PHILIPPIANS 4:19 KJV

Ryan and Brandi needed to move to a two-bedroom apartment; they prayed specifically for a monthly rent of $800.

The landlords at the apartments they liked discounted the regular $900 rent to $850. Although tempted to agree, Ryan and Brandi trusted God to answer their initial prayer. Within thirty minutes, the landlords called back; they liked them so much they agreed to the $800 rent.

Although you may not know how, God can answer your prayers.

You Don't Have to Solve Everyone's Problems

And let us consider how we may spur one another
on toward love and good deeds.

HEBREWS 10:24 NIV

I often think my way is the best and everyone should follow it. When a problem arises, if everyone listened to me, they'd be fine.

That's a rather lofty position to take. Solving everyone's problems isn't my job, particularly because I know only one side of the story. I cannot force anyone to choose God, but I can encourage people to move toward Him.

You Don't Have to Understand

Trust in the LORD with all thine heart;
and lean not unto thine own understanding.

PROVERBS 3:5 KJV

When Pastor Nate Ruch's son was a toddler, he gashed his forehead on a table. The ER was understaffed, so Pastor Nate had to hold David so the doctor could numb him before stitches. As David watched the needle come close, he was confused. *Dad, what are you doing to me?* He didn't understand; he had to trust his father.

We don't always understand God's actions, but we can be confident He knows what is best.

You Don't Have to Worry

Don't worry about anything; instead, pray about
everything. Tell God what you need,
and thank him for all he has done.

PHILIPPIANS 4:6 NLT

Have you ever noticed how your life stops when you are worried about something? Worry consumes your thoughts in an attempt to make the situation better.

But no amount of worry can alter circumstances. Only prayer can! Bring that situation to God and leave it with Him. You may need to mentally bring it to Him over and over, but do whatever it takes. Worry never works; prayer does.

You Don't Have to Wear Someone Else's Armor

Then Saul gave David his own armor. . . . "I can't go in these," [David] protested to Saul. "I'm not used to them." So David took them off again.
1 Samuel 17:38–39 NLT

We can easily assume people need to live and pray as we do, just as King Saul assumed David must dress for battle as he did.

Trust God to show you the path He wants you to walk. It may look different from others, but as long as it is aligned with God's Word, follow your heart.

SHARING JESUS

Able to Share Your Story

We will not hide these truths from our children;
we will tell the next generation about the
glorious deeds of the LORD, about his power
and his mighty wonders.

PSALM 78:4 NLT

Our friend Pastor Nate Ruch once said, "The stories your kids are hearing become their faith." It's true. My faith has been impacted greatly by watching people close to me live their faith. We should be open with our kids about what God is doing in our hearts. As Pastor Nate concluded, let people hear our story and not just our doctrine.

Able to Laugh

A merry heart doeth good like a medicine.
PROVERBS 17:22 KJV

My aunt Missy shines with God's love, partially because she can always laugh at herself. A favorite story was when she was driving a convertible through a cul-de-sac and recognized her friend's parents walking nearby. She couldn't remember their names, so she waved and yelled what she did remember. . .her own name. They looked at her oddly and smiled. Her embarrassment has become a story she loves to tell.

Go ahead and laugh at yourself; it's one way you can be a bright light for Jesus.

Able to Parent Well

Train up a child in the way he should go:
and when he is old, he will not depart from it.

PROVERBS 22:6 KJV

I don't have a temper, so it amazes me how quickly I can raise my voice with my kids. Usually it's just to get my point across because I'm not sure they will hear me or respond any other way.

Children require a lot of patience, multiple times a day. When I catch myself raising my voice, I try to stop and remember I can parent well. Parenting patiently, as best as possible, is one way I show God's love to my kids.

Able to Go Outside Your Comfort Zone

*"Go into all the world and preach
the Good News to everyone."*

Mark 16:15 NLT

My friend Colleen is quiet and reserved until she shares Jesus with others. One time, she walked up to a group of guys playing soccer. The ball came toward her. She stepped on it, encouraged the guys to come over, shared about Jesus, prayed with them, then let them continue their game.

Just as Colleen did, you can rely on the Holy Spirit to help you boldly share the Gospel with others.

Able to Reflect God's Love

Let us love one another, for love comes from God.
Everyone who loves has been born of God and
knows God. Whoever does not love does
not know God, because God is love.

1 JOHN 4:7–8 NIV

I once prayed for my husband to encounter God's love. Then I had a revelation: I am the way Erik sees God's love.

Although it's easy to feel inadequate to properly showcase God's love, that's exactly what we are called to do for others. We lean on Him, and He enables us to reflect His love.

Able to Find Them

*"But I say, wake up and look around.
The fields are already ripe for harvest."*
John 4:35 NLT

One day, we spent three hours hunting for the TV remote. We didn't know where to hunt, so we just did what we knew to do: clean, straighten, and go about our daily lives until it appeared.

Sometimes our Christian lives imitate this game of hide-and-seek. We don't know where to find unsaved people—but if we will keep our eyes open, God will bring them into our lives so we can minister to them!

Able to Brighten the World

*Ye are the light of the world. A city that is set on
an hill cannot be hid. . . . Let your light so shine
before men, that they may see your good works,
and glorify your Father which is in heaven.*

MATTHEW 5:14, 16 KJV

What happens when you turn a light on in a dark
room? Darkness has no option; it must leave.
When you shine your light for Jesus, darkness has
no option as well. It must leave. Go shine your
light to the world.

Able to Live Creatively

*Don't forget to pray for us, that God will open doors
for telling the mystery of Christ, even while I'm
locked up in this jail. Pray that every time I
open my mouth I'll be able to make
Christ plain as day to them.*

COLOSSIANS 4:3–4 MSG

Paul was in prison, yet he was still looking for ways
to share Jesus with other people. He probably had
to get creative in how he spread the news while
locked in jail. May his creativity inspire us to find
ways to spread God's Good News.

Able to See Their Need

*For the LORD gives wisdom; from his mouth
come knowledge and understanding.*
PROVERBS 2:6 NIV

A mom makes sure her kids are fed and well rested so they don't get crabby. A friend brings a meal to a grieving wife or lends a listening ear. A cousin calls to check on her family member whose parents just got divorced. One way we reflect Jesus to the world is by looking for other people's needs and doing everything we can to meet them.

Ask God: *whose need can I meet today?*

Able to Rescue Prodigals

My dear friends, if you know people who have wandered off from God's truth, don't write them off. Go after them. Get them back and you will have rescued precious lives from destruction and prevented an epidemic of wandering away from God.

JAMES 5:19–20 MSG

Have you ever had that moment when you read a friend's Facebook update and think, *Really? I thought they knew Jesus.* I am slowly learning not to judge in that moment of realization. Instead, I should point them back to Jesus in prayer, in action, and—if God leads—in word.

ENDURANCE

Immerse Yourself in God's Word

*I have hidden your word in my heart,
that I might not sin against you.*

PSALM 119:11 NLT

Enduring through difficulty can feel impossible, but it isn't. Read, study, or memorize God's Word, and give yourself ammunition to make it through difficult times.

When you are alone, the Holy Spirit can remind you of Hebrews 13:5. When you are scared, you'll remember Psalm 23. When you need healing, Isaiah 53:4–5 will come to mind. The Word of God is filled with power. It will strengthen you when you need it the most.

Immerse Yourself in Grace

"Don't pick on people, jump on their failures, criticize their faults—unless, of course, you want the same treatment. That critical spirit has a way of boomeranging."
MATTHEW 7:1–2 MSG

After hearing news that another celebrity marriage ended after only four years, I thought, *That's dumb.* Then I immediately heard inside me, *"That's difficult."*

God hasn't called me to judge other people's decisions. My job is to love them, recognize I don't understand their situation, and give them grace upon grace for what they are facing.

Immerse Yourself in Stories of Faith

Take the old prophets as your mentors. They put up with anything, went through everything, and never once quit, all the time honoring God.
JAMES 5:10–11 MSG

I always thought the Old Testament phrase "the God of Abraham, Isaac, and Jacob" was another name for God. It actually is an endurance principle in action. That phrase prompts people to remember what God has done for their faith heroes. If God can do it for Abraham, Isaac, and Jacob—and your parents, grandparents, or other faith heroes—He can do it for you!

Immerse Yourself in Discipline

Sin speaks a dead language that means nothing to you; God speaks your mother tongue, and you hang on every word.

ROMANS 6:10 MSG

Sometimes I feel like I don't have the ability to say no to my negative desires. Then one day I read what Paul wrote. I realized that I don't speak the language of sin anymore. When I accepted Christ into my life, I accepted a new standard of living—and the ability of God to help me live that way. He knows how to help me live disciplined before Him.

Immerse Yourself in Consistency

Do you see what this means—all these pioneers who blazed the way, all these veterans cheering us on? It means we'd better get on with it. Strip down, start running—and never quit!

HEBREWS 12:1 MSG

The past two seasons of the reality show *Ultimate Survival Alaska* have been won by the "Endurance Team." These endurance athletes pressed through the wild Alaskan terrain by packing light, traveling fast, and taking the longer, smarter path to bring them to the end.

In the same way, consistent, wise choices prepare us to win in life.

Immerse Yourself in Trust

For the word of the LORD holds true,
and we can trust everything he does.
PSALM 33:4 NLT

We just listed our old town house at a price less than we wanted to properly compete with another listing close-by. After working hard to turn our lived-in house to move-in ready, it was disappointing—but it isn't the end of the story. I have prayed for a specific selling price, and I will trust God for that to happen. So even when it's hard to trust, I encourage you to do the same.

Immerse Yourself in Radical Thinking

*"To you who are ready for the truth, I say this:
Love your enemies. Let them bring out the best
in you, not the worst. . . . Live generously."*

Luke 6:27–28, 30 MSG

"They bring out the worst in me." Although this phrase is common, when you're following Christ, it should not describe you. In fact, God wants the opposite to happen. Every time you see someone you're at odds with, let them bring out your best. Let your knowledge of God's love for them propel you to love them generously.

Immerse Yourself in Thankfulness

Thank God no matter what happens. This is the way God wants you who belong to Christ Jesus to live.

1 Thessalonians 5:18 msg

We're teaching our three-year-old he doesn't need to whine to get what he wants. Although he cried to get something as a baby, he's growing up. Whining is no longer appropriate.

As adults, our whining sounds more like complaining—and yes, it sounds like fingernails on a chalkboard whether you are three or forty-three. Instead of complaining, try thankfulness. It keeps God and all His good things in front of you.

Immerse Yourself in Good Friends

*Don't be fooled by those who say such things,
for "bad company corrupts good character."*
1 Corinthians 15:33 nlt

God's voice sometimes sounds like your mom, spouse, or best friend. If I have a hard time quieting down and listening to the Lord, I talk to my friends. They often know just how to encourage me, provide advice, or tell me I'm doing a good job. I've surrounded myself with good people so God has the opportunity to use them to bring good counsel into my life. I encourage you to do the same.

Immerse Yourself in Singing

*Sing to the LORD; praise his name. Each day
proclaim the good news that he saves.*
PSALM 96:2 NLT

Music affects us. That's why singing or dancing
quickly uplifts our spirits. More than once, I've
been walking down the street pondering my
problems and a song will come to my heart. The
song reminds me of exactly what I need in that
moment, whether it's a reminder that God is good
or everything will work out. Since songs provide
the background for your life, why not make sure
that background will strengthen you in your faith?

Immerse Yourself in Good Thinking

Fix your thoughts on what is true, and honorable,
and right, and pure, and lovely, and admirable.
Think about things that are excellent
and worthy of praise.

PHILIPPIANS 4:8 NLT

Our thoughts indicate the direction our life will take. That's why I am continually attempting to train my mind to think beneficial thoughts. When I start to get angry, I count in my head. When I'm doing something boring, I focus on the finish line.

I encourage you to ask the Lord to help you keep your mind and heart on Him.

Immerse Yourself in Rest

"Are you tired? Worn out? Burned out on religion?
Come to me. Get away with me and you'll recover
your life. I'll show you how to take a real rest. . . .
Keep company with me and you'll learn
to live freely and lightly."
MATTHEW 11:28–30 MSG

Recently, I found myself exhausted because of too much to do in too little time with too much strain on my emotions. Then I remembered where my true strength comes from.

If you need strength, ask God to show you how to put Matthew 11:28–30 into practice.

FAITH

He Is at Work

Even though on the outside it often looks like things are falling apart on us, on the inside, where God is making new life, not a day goes by without his unfolding grace.

2 Corinthians 4:16 MSG

Every Christmas Eve as a child, I was excited to go to bed. I knew the presents under our Christmas tree would grow overnight. My parents worked while I slept to surprise me and my brother.

In the same way, you won't always see God at work, but as you trust Him, know change is on the way.

He Is Our Healer

By [Jesus'] stripes ye were healed.
1 PETER 2:24 KJV

The summer after my three-year-old had been born, I went to see the doctor about recurring shooting pain in my wrists. I was shocked when the doctor determined the solution was surgery. I walked away resolved to pray about the advice before making a decision.

Sure enough, the Great Physician provided an answer. In the following months, the pain stopped, and I haven't had any for years.

God doesn't favor one person over another. If He can heal me, He can heal you too.

He Is Omniscient

And there came a voice to him, Rise, Peter; kill, and eat. But Peter said, Not so, Lord; for I have never eaten any thing that is common or unclean. And the voice spake unto him again the second time, What God hath cleansed, that call not thou common.
ACTS 10:13–15 KJV

God directed Peter to do something different from what was religiously acceptable. If God asks you to do something you don't understand, obey anyway. Just as Peter did, you'll get to live out your part of God's greater plan on this earth.

He Is Flexible

Wait on the Lord: be of good courage, and he shall strengthen thine heart: wait, I say, on the Lord.
PSALM 27:14 KJV

Religion says we must have a quiet time of thirty minutes every morning to grow close to God, but God is flexible. If reading the Bible in the morning is intimidating, try reading in the afternoon or evening. Listen to the Bible while driving. Read this devotional while waiting for an oil change.

Whatever you do, keep your goal in mind: being continually aware of and strengthening your relationship with God.

He Is Holy

*But as he which hath called you is holy, so be ye holy
in all manner of conversation; because it is
written, Be ye holy; for I am holy.*
1 Peter 1:15–16 KJV

Focusing on God's grace and forgiveness can cause us to forget that God is holy and without blame. He is perfect in all His ways and calls us to move in that direction of holiness.

We can't become holy in our own strength, but by His grace, we can acknowledge His holiness and strive to become more like Him.

He Is Our Friend

And so it happened just as the Scriptures say:
"Abraham believed God, and God counted him as
righteous because of his faith." He was
even called the friend of God.

JAMES 2:23 NLT

You can tell God secrets and complain about life. You can praise Him and ask Him to change things. Isn't it amazing that we can confidently approach God, update Him on life, turn to Him in need, and trust Him through thick and thin? He can be—and wants to be!—your best friend.

He Is Above All

God sits above the circle of the earth.
The people below seem like grasshoppers
to him! He spreads out the heavens like
a curtain and makes his tent from them.

ISAIAH 40:22 NLT

Some days I see life from God's perspective. My problems are microscopic and His power is prevalent. Other days I'm overwhelmed by what I'm facing just as an ant may feel walking through a cornfield.

When you're stuck seeing life through your perspective, imagine the Lord on His heavenly throne. Picture the realities of His power. That perspective will change your life.

He Is Faithful

God will do this, for he is faithful to do what he says,
and he has invited you into partnership
with his Son, Jesus Christ our Lord.
1 Corinthians 1:9 nlt

Difficult times can cause us to forget what God has done for us. Our minds think, *Well, this situation is different. I don't know how He'll do it.* The truth is, the situation you are facing right now isn't too big for God. Nothing is impossible for Him. He has proven faithful to believers for thousands of years. He will prove Himself faithful to you.

He Is Our Shelter

The Lord is my rock, my fortress, and my savior;
my God is my rock, in whom I find protection.
He is my shield, the power that saves
me, and my place of safety.

PSALM 18:2 NLT

Have you ever looked outside the window to realize it was raining hard—and you had no idea because you were sheltered inside your house or office? When we're in God's family, He does that for us. He protects us from getting wet in the rains of life, even when we are unaware He's there. Isn't that awesome?

He Is Our Refuge

God is our refuge and strength,
always ready to help in times of trouble.

PSALM 46:1 NLT

The phone call that brings bad news. The moment something feels physically wrong in your body. The call from the banker, principal, police officer, or another authority figure that signals impending doom.

Every time you face these situations, you have a refuge. You have somewhere you can run and hide. You can cry, whine, pray, and rest and do whatever you need to do during difficulty. Stay in your Father's arms.

He Is Forever

*The grass withereth, and the flower thereof falleth
away: but the word of the Lord endureth for ever.*
1 PETER 1:24–25 KJV

Have you ever tried to find an end to a circle? How
about the beginning? Of course, you know you
can't find either. In the same way, God is eternal.
He has no beginning and no end. Actually, Revelation, chapter 22, says that Jesus *is* the beginning
and the end. His words will stand true forever;
He cannot lie. Everything about Him lasts. What
a wonderful promise from our Savior!

He Is Forever Yours

For He has said, "I will never [under any circumstances] desert you [nor give you up nor leave you without support, nor will I in any degree leave you helpless], nor will I forsake or let you down or relax My hold on you [assuredly not]!"
HEBREWS 13:5 AMP

Everything about God is eternal, including His goodness and love. When we receive God's love and place ourselves right in the middle of His hand, He will never relax His hold on us. What an amazing truth!

He Is Glorious

*We saw it with our own eyes: Jesus resplendent with
light from God the Father as the voice of Majestic
Glory spoke: "This is my Son, marked by my love,
focus of all my delight." We were there on the holy
mountain with him. We heard the voice
out of heaven with our very own ears.*

2 PETER 1:16–18 MSG

Imagine that moment Jesus was "resplendent
with light." It was an out-of-the-ordinary display
of God's glory that showed the world the God
we serve is beautiful, glorious, and beyond our
comprehension. He deserves our praise.

He Is Love

"For God so loved the world, that he gave his only Son, that whoever believes in him should not perish but have eternal life."

JOHN 3:16 ESV

God's greatest act of love was sending His own Son to the earth to die for our sins. He made a way for you to live with Him forever. If you ever need to be reassured of His love for you, meditate on this truth.

He Is Patient

The Lord is not slow to fulfill his promise as some
count slowness, but is patient toward you,
not wishing that any should perish,
but that all should reach repentance.

2 PETER 3:9 ESV

Sometimes when I get frustrated with other people, I remember God is patient with me. If He can be patient through all my ups and downs, I can be patient with those around me. A quick prayer and a deep breath help me refocus and remember that no matter what someone has done, I can find a way to be patient with them.

He Is the Way

Jesus told him, "I am the way, the truth, and the life.
No one can come to the Father except through me."

Worship music, church services, and Bible studies
are not the way to your freedom. They are tools
to point you toward Jesus. Sometimes we forget
that simple truth and get caught up in the rituals
of Christianity. Jesus is the way to forgiveness,
health, and restoration. He is our access to God's
love, mercy, and grace. The only way we receive
God's gifts is through Jesus.

He Is Mighty

*"I am the Alpha and the Omega—the beginning
and the end," says the Lord God. "I am the one
who is, who always was, and who is still
to come—the Almighty One."*

REVELATION 1:8 NLT

God created the universe. He created human
beings. He created every atom that exists in this
universe. He is powerful, unfathomable, and
limitless.

This same God brings His might and power to
our situations and applies them in gentle ways.
He loves us unconditionally.

Let your worries wash away knowing He is
bigger than everything you face.

He Is Our Protector

The LORD says, "I will rescue those who love me.
I will protect those who trust in my name."
PSALM 91:14 NLT

Recently, my husband was hanging shelving in our garage when a piece pulled away from the wall. As a result, he crashed about four feet to the cement floor. Thanks to the metal shelving on the ground and the angels and grace of God, he walked away with only a bruised forearm and the need for a chiropractor visit.

Be at peace. God is watching over you and protecting your every step.

He Is Just

*In his justice he will pay back
those who persecute you.*

2 Thessalonians 1:6 nlt

It's hard to watch suffering happen. It's hard to experience it ourselves. Even more than both of those, it's hard when you wonder where God is in the middle of it.

That's when we need to remind ourselves that He is just. Although He is infinite love, His love is just. Rest in that fact: He knows how to handle His people. He knows how to respond to evil. He knows what He is doing because He is God.

He Is Merciful

*But God, who is rich in mercy, for his great love
wherewith he loved us, even when we were dead in
sins, hath quickened us together with Christ. . .
and hath raised us up together, and made us sit
together in heavenly places in Christ Jesus.*
EPHESIANS 2:4–6 KJV

We don't deserve God's love, yet God views us
as worthy through the sacrifice of His Son. He
forgives our sins time and again. He allows us to
keep coming to Him despite our downfalls and
gives us a path to freedom and success in life.
Let's be grateful for His mercy!

CHRISTIAN LIVING

Fight Fair

*My dear children, let's not just talk about love;
let's practice real love.*
1 JOHN 3:18 MSG

When you disagree with someone, always remember to fight fair. Make sure you each understand the "playing field": You love each other, want what is best for that relationship, and consider each other equals. You simply disagree.

When you fight fair, you value the other person through your words, your tone, your attitude, and even your actions while you disagree. So fight well, and fight fair.

Fight Distraction

*Their loyalty is divided between God
and the world, and they are unstable
in everything they do.*

JAMES 1:8 NLT

From friends and family to media and social media,
a lot of voices in this world are clamoring for your
attention. If you listen to them, you will find your
life to be unstable. Aim to keep your ears tuned
in to the voice that matters most: our heavenly
Father. As you tune in to Him and tune out others,
you'll hear the Lord's voice more clearly.

Fight Regret

But if we confess our sins to him,
he is faithful and just to forgive us our sins
and to cleanse us from all wickedness.

1 JOHN 1:9 NLT

Regret keeps us feeling unworthy before God. It keeps us focused on something other than how much God loves us. We can expand and increase our ability to receive personally from the Lord when we think more about Him, but that's not possible when we're focused on past mistakes.

Today, move your thoughts away from things you've done wrong; instead, focus on God's love for you.

Fight Unforgiveness

"But when you are praying, first forgive anyone you are holding a grudge against, so that your Father in heaven will forgive your sins, too."

MARK 11:25 NLT

It can be hard to let go when others have hurt you. You want to relive what they've done and how justified you are in your frustration against them. But holding a grudge gets you nowhere. In fact, answered prayers only come when you've first forgiven.

Forgiving others is our way of acknowledging how God first forgave us.

Fight Segregation

You do well when you complete the Royal Rule of
the Scriptures: "Love others as you love yourself."
But if you play up to these so-called important
people, you go against the Rule
and stand convicted by it.

JAMES 2:8–9 MSG

Jesus never ignored a leper coming to Him, even
if the leper looked disgusting due to his disease.
If He had thoughts of disgust when looking at a
person, He always chose love. It's a good reminder
that even when a person doesn't look or act like
we want, we are still called to love.

Fight the Enemy

For we are not fighting against flesh-and-blood enemies, but against evil rulers and authorities of the unseen world, against mighty powers in this dark world, and against evil spirits in the heavenly places.

EPHESIANS 6:12 NLT

We often focus our mental energies and frustrations on the people around us since we interact regularly with them—yet they are not our enemy. Our enemy is Satan and his cohorts. Whenever people frustrate us, step back. No person is our enemy. Instead, look to God, and He will give you wisdom for the situation you face.

Fight Too Many Options

*He makes the whole body fit together perfectly.
As each part does its own special work, it helps the
other parts grow, so that the whole body is
healthy and growing and full of love.*
EPHESIANS 4:16 NLT

Currently, new churches are popping up all over America. This trend is wonderful because it brings a small church atmosphere within a short driving distance of people everywhere. The problem for Christians is that it can create too many options. God wants us to connect to a specific local church and stay there. Pray that He leads you to the right church.

Fight Compromise

*Therefore, I have set my face like a stone,
determined to do his will. And I know
that I will not be put to shame.*

Isaiah 50:7 NLT

Some days it's easy to be lazy. I know I have a good relationship with God, so sometimes I play on my iPad a few more minutes before reading my Bible. The reality, though, is that my "good" relationship can grow from good to great—and beyond!

Let's become determined to push past what's easy and lean on God to help us read the Word, pray, and grow in Him!

Fight Closed Ears

My child, listen and be wise:
keep your heart on the right course.
PROVERBS 23:19 NLT

Recently, my husband wanted me to make cookies with him. Based on my lengthy to-do list, I said no. After two more attempts, he said, "I was trying to relive some of our memories baking together in the kitchen."

Being too busy with good things is an easy trap to fall into, so resolve to take time to listen to cues from your family and friends. If they need you, put them first.

Fight Sin

Sin speaks a dead language that means nothing to you; God speaks your mother tongue, and you hang on every word. . . .That means you must not give sin a vote in the way you conduct your lives.
ROMANS 6:10, 12 MSG

It's easy to have excuses as to why we keep doing things that don't please God. *I can't change. . . . It's not really sin. . . . I do enough other good things.* The reality, though, is that as daughters of God, our nature is to act as God wants. God's grace can help us choose wisely.

VICTORY

We Are Not Condemned

*There is therefore now no condemnation to them
which are in Christ Jesus, who walk not after
the flesh, but after the Spirit.*
ROMANS 8:1 KJV

I admit, some days I eat all the junk food I want,
feel crabby, and generally don't make good decisions. By night, it's usually more difficult to read
my Bible because I feel condemned.

The good news is, no matter how much I mess
up, I can still approach God—and you can too!
He provides each one of us with the strength we
need to do better tomorrow.

We Are to Live in the Spirit

But you are not controlled by your sinful nature.
You are controlled by the Spirit if you have
the Spirit of God living in you.

ROMANS 8:9 NLT

Sometimes I feel like I can't win. I agree with Paul's thoughts in Romans 7: I do what I don't want and don't do what I do want. I have to remember, though, that God has given me a new nature. It's my job to choose His nature over sin. When I do, I live where God wants me to—in His Spirit!

We Are Adopted

For ye have not received the spirit of bondage again to fear; but ye have received the Spirit of adoption, whereby we cry, Abba, Father.
ROMANS 8:15 KJV

When a child is adopted, she takes on her new family's name, status, relatives, and resources. In the same way, when we step into God's family, we become part of a new family. We have a heavenly Father who backs us up with His ability, power, strength, and glory. Everything that is His is ours because we are adopted as His kids!

We Are Called

*And we know that all things work together for good
to them that love God, to them who are
the called according to his purpose.*

ROMANS 8:28 KJV

Romans 8:28 is a wonderful verse to rest in when difficulty comes: God brings good out of every situation we face. Sometimes the good is not easily seen, but if you tune your heart to hear God's whisper, you'll be able to find His hand constantly at work behind the scenes.

We Are His Heirs

"The son said, 'Look how many years I've stayed here serving you, never giving you one moment of grief, but have you ever thrown a party for me and my friends? . . . .' His father said, 'Son, you don't understand. You're with me all the time, and everything that is mine is yours.'"
Luke 15:29, 31 MSG

It can be easy to complain when those who go astray get more attention than us. The reality, though, is that God's resources are already ours! We don't need a party; we have Him.

We Are Loved

*For I am persuaded, that neither death, nor life, nor
angels, nor principalities, nor powers, nor things
present, nor things to come, nor height, nor depth,
nor any other creature, shall be able to separate
us from the love of God, which is in
Christ Jesus our Lord.*
ROMANS 8:38–39 KJV

I think through life in terms of conditions, excuses,
and reasons as to why I can or can't do certain
things. God thinks with only one condition in mind:
love. He loves you; He loves me. He exudes love.
Be confident in that fact!

We Outnumber Them

"When you go out to battle against your enemies and see horses and chariots and people more numerous than you, do not be afraid of them; for the LORD your God, who brought you up from the land of Egypt, is with you."

DEUTERONOMY 20:1 AMP

Anyone who attempts to battle God will be sorely disappointed. Remember what happened when Elisha prayed for his servant's eyes to be opened? He saw the hills were filled with horses and chariots of fire (see 2 Kings 6:17). God's resources aren't always seen, but they are there!

We Are Victorious for a Reason

But thanks be to God, who always leads us in
triumph in Christ, and through us spreads and makes
evident everywhere the sweet fragrance
of the knowledge of Him.
2 CORINTHIANS 2:14 AMP

As soon as a victory of any sort occurs in your country, what happens? The news spreads quickly. Victory tells a story that compels people to listen.

In the same way, God wants our personal lives to be a banner of victory for Him that draws people into His kingdom!

We Are on the Winning Side

"Be courageous [be confident, be undaunted,
be filled with joy]; I have overcome the world."
[My conquest is accomplished,
My victory abiding.]

JOHN 16:33 AMP

When we are part of God's kingdom, the world and its tricks no longer have power to change our lives. The problem is, we give the world power by giving it our attention and time. So don't allow that to happen. Remember: we are on the winning side!

We Wait on God

The horse is prepared for the day of battle,
but the victory belongs to the LORD.
PROVERBS 21:31 NLT

As Christians, we plan our lives the way we think they should play out. The reality, though, is that we can prepare all day long, but in the end, the path to victory is given by the Lord. As the *Message* version of Proverbs 21:31 says, "Do your best, prepare for the worst—then trust GOD to bring victory."

LOVE

Be Patient

*Love endures with patience
and serenity, love is kind.*
1 Corinthians 13:4 amp

God's unending patience amazes me. He loves us through ups, downs, twists, turns, and every hormone change in our bodies. He is endless in how He loves us—which means He is endless in His patience.

I often come to the end of my rope with people. The questions are endless. *Why can't they just act differently? Why can't they understand?* Then I remember how patient God is with me. If He can be patient with my troubles, I can be patient with others.

Be Kind

Instead, be kind to each other, tenderhearted,
forgiving one another, just as God
through Christ has forgiven you.
EPHESIANS 4:32 NLT

Although the battles of life ebb and flow, you will constantly come in contact with people who are facing a difficult battle that you know nothing about. That's why kindness is important. You never know how opening the door for someone or smiling at a stranger will affect that person's day. Sometimes it could be just the emotional boost another person needs. That's why kindness is key.

Be Humble

Don't be selfish; don't try to impress others.
Be humble, thinking of others
as better than yourselves.

PHILIPPIANS 2:3 NLT

Humility is one way we show love to each other. When we are humble, we value others before our own opinion. We recognize that we don't know everything. We know that we may be good at something, but we don't flaunt it. We just do what we have been called to do and support others along the way.

More than anything, we know that without God, we are nothing, but with Him, we can do all things.

Be Slow to Anger

Be ye angry, and sin not.
EPHESIANS 4:26 KJV

"The sellers aren't going to pay for anything we listed from the inspection." I was shocked at Erik's comment. Negotiation and compromise are part of buying a home; their rude response made me want to give up on the home entirely—but I knew that acting out of anger would get us nowhere. Instead, I waited.

Nighttime came; my anger subsided. I knew the house was perfect for my family; the anger was simply a detour from God's plan.

Don't act out of anger. Show love instead.

Be Thoughtful

We should help others do what is right and build them up in the Lord.

<small>ROMANS 15:2 NLT</small>

Before I post on social media, I often ask myself, *Why am I posting this?* If it's to brag, shame, or stir controversy, it isn't worth it. When I post something, I want it to be for one purpose: to encourage or inform others. For example, I have a few family members who look forward to seeing photos of my boys, so I post in an effort to bring smiles to their faces.

Loving others involves thinking of them first.

Be Full of Trust

Love. . .believes all things
[looking for the best in each one].
1 CORINTHIANS 13:7 AMP

Trusting everyone at all times borders on naivete. Believing the best in others should be considered from this triangle of trust: You first trust God for wisdom; He, in turn, will provide you with peace and direction as to whom you can trust. When you come across someone with wrong intentions, He will ensure you know not to move forward in that relationship.

Trusting God provides us with the grace and ability to trust others.

Be Aware of Imperfections

For now [in this time of imperfection] we see in a mirror dimly [a blurred reflection, a riddle, an enigma], but then [when the time of perfection comes we will see reality] face to face.
1 Corinthians 13:12 AMP

All too often I've seen Christians bombard other Christians for their faith. They disagree with an angle of their beliefs that doesn't affect their eternal salvation and verbally fight about it. I find that a waste of time. Loving others involves realizing it's okay when our interpretations of the Bible vary.

Be Compassionate

"Love your enemies! Do good to them. . . . Be compassionate, just as your Father is compassionate."

LUKE 6:35–36 NLT

I think these two verses are juxtaposed, because you can't love your enemies unless you have compassion for what they are going through. They may have lost a parent when they were young or been abused. Our enemies often have reasons for the hatred they feel today. Being compassionate toward them allows them to see themselves as God does: sinners who are misled and haven't yet fully understood God's love.

Be a Good Listener

Post this at all the intersections,
dear friends: Lead with your ears.
JAMES 1:19 MSG

Last night, I had three conversations. Two were with new neighbors and one was with my husband. Because my husband and I talk all the time, I realized I was less quick to turn my attention away from my to-do list to listen to him than I was with my neighbors.

If we truly want to love our friends and family well, we will learn to consistently put all distractions aside and listen to them.

Be Clothed in Love

Above all, clothe yourselves with love,
which binds us all together in perfect harmony.
COLOSSIANS 3:14 NLT

As we all know, clothing is a good thing. It protects us from the elements and from strange looks. Without it, we would be more sensitive to the heat or cold and become burned by the sun and wind. With it, we are strong and confident stepping out to approach the day.

In the same way, walking in love keeps us confident, protected, and more sensitive to God than the elements of this life. Put your love cloak on today!

PRODUCTIVITY

The Power of a Minute

So be careful how you live. . . .
Make the most of every opportunity.
EPHESIANS 5:15–16 NLT

Recently, God pulled me away from my work and said, *"Spend time with Me."* Although I was nervous about spending time away from what I needed to get done, I did it. I had an awesome time in His presence—and I was surprised to discover it had only been ten minutes.

So don't fret about what you can't give; give God what you can. Every minute you give Him your focused attention has the power to change your life.

The Power of a Pause

And "don't sin by letting anger control you."
Don't let the sun go down while you are still angry,
for anger gives a foothold to the devil.
EPHESIANS 4:26–27 NLT

Whether it's potty training a toddler (yikes!) or dealing with coworkers, people test our patience all the time. One key to dealing with that frustration is learning to pause. Take a breath when you feel anger rise inside you. Gather your thoughts and settle your heart so you don't act out of anger.

The Power of Perspective

"[Do not] worry about everyday life—whether you have enough food and drink, or enough clothes to wear. Isn't life more than food, and your body more than clothing?"

MATTHEW 6:25 NLT

Recently, I became overwhelmed by my messy house and massive amounts of laundry. To top it off, my underwire bra had gone through the dryer—a no-no to keep it looking nice.

Then my exhaustion turned into an epiphany. The bra provided perspective: if that's all I have to worry about—a messy house and a not-as-nice bra—I'm in a good place.

The Power of Paper Plates

You are not your own, for you were bought with a price. So glorify God in your body.
1 CORINTHIANS 6:19–20 ESV

It's easy to get so caught up in a cycle of attempting perfection that we forget it's okay to relax.

Currently, I'm enjoying the batch of paper plates we have in the cabinet. They provide a break from the endless cycle of washing dishes and putting them away. And you know what? Eliminating stress strengthens our bodies—and God likes it when we take care of ourselves and relax!

The Power of Balance

For everything there is a season,
and a time for every matter under heaven.
ECCLESIASTES 3:1 ESV

Once I made banana bread with four bananas. The problem was, the recipe called for three bananas. I figured the additional fruit would be fine, but I was wrong. The final product was mushy and hadn't cooked properly due to the unbalanced proportions.

It's a great reminder that God wants our lives to be balanced. We can't spend our lives solely reading the Bible or washing dishes. We need to give ourselves grace and time to stay balanced.

The Power of Doing "Nothing"

One thing have I desired of the Lord, that will I seek after; that I may dwell in the house of the Lord all the days of my life, to behold the beauty of the Lord, and to enquire in his temple.

PSALM 27:4 KJV

Because technology has us constantly doing multiple things at once, quiet times with God can sometimes feel unproductive. The reality, though, is that our quiet time with God is the most productive thing we can do—being with our Savior and learning what He has planned for that day.

The Power of Creativity

"And he has filled him with the Spirit of God, with skill, with intelligence, with knowledge, and with all craftsmanship, to devise artistic designs, to work in gold and silver and bronze."

EXODUS 35:31–32 ESV

One day, I realized the kids needed "food" for their outdoor playhouse. I looked on Craigslist, not wanting to spend money. Then God gave me a creative idea. Use the toys we already had!

When you're stuck in the middle of not knowing what to do, ask God for a creative idea, and He will come through!

The Power of a Shower

Now to Him who is able to [carry out His purpose and] do superabundantly more than all that we dare ask or think [infinitely beyond our greatest prayers, hopes, or dreams].

EPHESIANS 3:20 AMP

Taking a shower is more than a chore to me; it's time I can spend imagining my future! If God can do more than I will ever think, I want to start dreaming big. You can too!

The Power of a Plan

*"For which of you, desiring to build
a tower, does not first sit down and
count the cost, whether he has
enough to complete it?"*

Luke 14:28 ESV

Potty training Brayden was tough. I had the beginning of a plan to get him going, but a week went by with limited results. My frustration led to creating a consistent, daylong plan. After a few days of that plan, Brayden was trained.

So always remember: Having a plan gives you easy-to-follow action steps that will bring the change you want.

The Power of Simplicity

*[Christ] is about to break into the open with his rule,
so proclaim the Message with intensity; keep on
your watch. Challenge, warn, and urge your people.
Don't ever quit. Just keep it simple.*

2 TIMOTHY 4:1–2 MSG

It's easy to complicate life. We have a list of things
we want to do for God, for ourselves, and for
others. It's important to remember to keep it
simple. Simplicity works; be persistent in simplicity
and you will win every time.

SELF-ESTEEM

Embrace Your Body

I will praise thee; for I am fearfully
and wonderfully made: marvellous are
thy works; and that my soul
knoweth right well.
PSALM 139:14 KJV

I remember when two moms commented to me on my flat, pre-kids stomach. "Our tummies only curve out now."

After three births, I also have the same pouch! I don't love my "mom bod"—and I'll ideally whip it into a different shape than the roundish one it is now—but I am in love with my kids. Because of that, I'll embrace every curve in my God-given body.

Embrace Correction

*All scripture is given by inspiration
of God, and is profitable for doctrine,
for reproof, for correction,
for instruction in righteousness.*
2 TIMOTHY 3:16 KJV

Sunday mornings are a time when the Word of God actively admonishes us to change so we can become more like Jesus. Sometimes, though, I focus too much on my wrongdoings and let conviction become guilt and shame. When I get overwhelmed by these feelings, I remember that correction helps me change. It provides the pressure I need to become a beautiful, multifaceted, sparkly diamond in God's kingdom.

Embrace Your Place

The human body has many parts, but the many parts make up one whole body. So it is with the body of Christ. . . . Our bodies have many parts, and God has put each part just where he wants it.

1 Corinthians 12:12, 18 NLT

As self-declared introverts with good social skills, my dad's sisters sometimes tell each other, "We must be toes in the body of Christ. . .and that's okay!" They've embraced their places ministering God's love to their families, friends, and whomever God brings across their paths.

May we imitate that simple perspective.

Embrace Your Partner

"But the Helper (Comforter, Advocate, Intercessor—Counselor, Strengthener, Standby), the Holy Spirit, whom the Father will send in My name. . .
He will teach you all things."
JOHN 14:26 AMP

Did you know that the Holy Spirit wants to partner with you in this life? He may not always give the answer to everything you ask when you want or expect it—but He will always supply you with what He knows you need, and He will always give you an answer on time. It's your job to trust Him.

Embrace God's Favor

And the king granted these requests,
because the gracious hand of God was on me.

NEHEMIAH 2:8 NLT

When Nehemiah heard about the ruins in which Jerusalem lay, he was distressed. As the king's cupbearer, he couldn't do anything immediately, except pray. When he was able to bring his concern to the king, Nehemiah was prepared. To some people's surprise, the king granted his request and allowed him to go to Jerusalem.

When you bring concerns before the Lord, He will pave the way for the same type of favor to be in your life.

Embrace Peace

Tell God what you need, and thank him for all he has done. Then you will experience God's peace, which exceeds anything we can understand. His peace will guard your hearts and minds as you live in Christ Jesus.

PHILIPPIANS 4:6–7 NLT

Do you want to live confidently? Pray about decisions you make, and then learn how to follow God's peace that's inside of you. When you have that moment when you know where God's peace is leading, anchor yourself in that moment. It will hold you through whatever life brings your way.

Embrace Your Weaknesses

*I am glad to boast about my weaknesses, so that the
power of Christ can work through me.*
2 Corinthians 12:9 NLT

Five years of living on my own didn't cause me to
meet my neighbors. My husband did. The reason
is, I'm an introvert who focuses mostly on com-
pleting projects. My husband loves connecting
with people!

I embrace the fact that I'm not a people person,
but I don't do this by ignoring people. I do it by
asking God to help me grow in that area. When
I am weak, He can be strong!

Embrace New Direction

For everything there is a season,
and a time for every matter under heaven.
ECCLESIASTES 3:1 ESV

When my friend discovered I moved forty minutes farther away from her, she replied, "Fun! Life is filled with new direction and opportunities. Since the only thing sure in life is change, one of the best things we can do is love and support our friends and family on their new adventures."

I admire how she embraced the change. Her final statement was endearing: "Distance can't close the door on dear friendships; it opens the door to new memories."

Embrace Apparent Insignificance

"I tell you the truth, unless a kernel of wheat is planted in the soil and dies, it remains alone. But its death will produce many new kernels— a plentiful harvest of new lives."

JOHN 12:24 NLT

Seeds are small, easy to lose, and do nothing until planted. In the same way, the things we do that glorify God can blossom into harvests much bigger than we ever imagine. A smile, a nice email or text, or a phone call to a friend—these things may sound small, but all have potential to impact someone's life for eternity.

Embrace Your Personality

Therefore, accept each other just as
Christ has accepted you so that
God will be given glory.
ROMANS 15:7 NLT

Have you noticed how every other week or so
you see a quiz or blog post on social media about
characteristics of an extrovert versus an introvert?
My aunt explained the difference well. If she and
my uncle drove past a neighbor whose back was
turned to them, she would keep driving. My uncle
would honk the horn and say hello.

Introvert or extrovert, God's plan includes you
being you.

STRENGTH TO STAND OUT

Free to Be Strong

*I pray that from his glorious, unlimited resources
he will empower you with inner strength
through his Spirit.*

Ephesians 3:16 nlt

Sometimes God needs us to stand up and speak truth to the world, whether through an individual relationship, a blog post, or some type of volunteer opportunity. Often, though, upholding truth takes the strength of Jesus to make it happen.

When you are facing something that feels outside of your strength, look to His power within. He will fuel His will to be done in your life.

Free to Be Settled

Then Christ will make his home in
your hearts as you trust in him.
EPHESIANS 3:17 NLT

I love the settled feeling that comes when everything is "right" in my world. Sometimes I have that same feeling when life is rough, but I feel odd when I do. The thought, *I should be worried*, creeps in—but it doesn't have to stay. We can trust God through thick and thin and live in a peace we will never understand despite everything we see. We can be settled in Him. . .period.

Free to Be Loved

*Your roots will grow down into God's
love and keep you strong.*

EPHESIANS 3:17 NLT

Understanding how much God loves you is foundational to a strong, godly lifestyle. Sometimes it can be hard to accept that love. We know everything we have done wrong; as a result, we assume we can't be loved.

The secret, though, is that God loves us anyway. He loves us at our worst and He loves us at our best. We are free to live life, knowing we are accepted and loved by Him.

Free to Experience Good Things

May you experience the love of Christ, though it is too great to understand fully. Then you will be made complete with all the fullness of life and power that comes from God.

EPHESIANS 3:19 NLT

God wants us to actually experience His love. When I show love to those around me, I know it involves lavishing good things on them, both in word and deed. God is the same way; He wants to give you good things and let you truly experience a life led by His love.

Free to Be Gobsmacked

Now all glory to God, who is able, through his mighty power at work within us, to accomplish infinitely more than we might ask or think.

EPHESIANS 3:20 NLT

The dictionary defines *gobsmacked* as "utterly astonished" or "astounded." I think those are great definitions of what God wants to do in our lives. He wants us to be overwhelmed by His goodness. He will meet both our big desires and our little ones. He'll even fulfill that secret wish you tucked safely away in your heart, all so you can know that you are loved.

Free to Be a Woman

A good woman is hard to find,
and worth far more than diamonds.
PROVERBS 31:10 MSG

You and I can embrace our womanhood. We are emotional; we aren't quite as physically strong as men. We can multitask like none other. The reason we can do these things is because God made us different from men, and that's okay.

The best part is, if you are a little stronger than your husband, God made *you* that way. Be confident in your womanhood—and be confident in what makes your womanhood uniquely you.

Free to Be You

*When they measure themselves by themselves
and compare themselves with themselves,
they lack wisdom and behave like fools.*

2 Corinthians 10:12 amp

Two weeks living in our new home and I'm still surrounded by boxes. My friend, on the other hand, said her new home was unpacked in two days. "We're just that crazy about not having a mess."

Although I would love an unpacked house, I'm unpacking my way—slowly but surely.

We all have different personalities, schedules, and tendencies. Don't compare yours to others'; simply embrace what you've been given.

Free to Be Confident

I pray that your hearts will be flooded with light so that you can understand the confident hope he has given to those he called—his holy people who are his rich and glorious inheritance.

EPHESIANS 1:18 NLT

God is love. He is forever with us. He is gracious and just. He wrote down all His promises in a book so we could have direction for our lives on this earth. He is unchangeable and all-powerful. In other words—you can be confident in His Word and in Him.

Free to Be Courageous

"This is my command—be strong and courageous!
Do not be afraid or discouraged. For the Lord
your God is with you wherever you go."

Joshua 1:9 nlt

Have you ever noticed trash on a sidewalk that hundreds walked by but no one picked up? Probably no one wanted to stand out in the crowd by doing something unusual.

God wants us to be the ones who courageously stand apart from everyone else and make a difference in this world. This kind of courage creates space for God to move in our lives.

Free to Be Led

*"After he has gathered his own flock,
he walks ahead of them, and they follow him
because they know his voice."*

JOHN 10:4 NLT

A relative of my husband lives down the street from our new house. One day I was driving home and felt the Spirit prompt me to drive by the neighboring houses I hadn't yet seen. When I got to her house, she was outside and we were able to meet.

We can be free to follow God's promptings because we know He has our best interests in mind.

OUR PROTECTION

Arm Yourself with Salvation

Truth, righteousness, peace, faith, and salvation are more than words. Learn how to apply them. You'll need them throughout your life.
EPHESIANS 6:14–17 MSG

Our salvation is much more than eternity spent with God, although that would be enough. God has provided us with armor that enables us to live this life well.

How do we put on the first piece, the helmet of salvation? We fill our minds with what God says about our lives. We read the Bible! It provides us with a mind-set that will help us live life God's way.

Arm Yourself with Truth

So stand firm and hold your ground, having
tightened the wide band of truth (personal integrity,
moral courage) around your waist.
EPHESIANS 6:14 AMP

Have you noticed how often you see conflicting articles? Someone says you should vaccinate your children; someone else says you shouldn't. Both of them have doctors backing up what they say. What should you believe?

The Word of God. Sure, it doesn't talk directly about vaccinations, but it does talk about wisdom, healing, and hearing God's voice. Listen to your heart, and God will guide you through your decisions.

Arm Yourself with Righteousness

*So stand firm and hold your
ground. . .having put on the breastplate
of righteousness (an upright heart).*
EPHESIANS 6:14 AMP

Jesus' selfless act of dying on the cross made me righteous before God. No dart of the enemy can penetrate my heart or shake that truth from my life because I'm wearing the breastplate of righteousness.

If you don't yet have assurance that God has made you righteous before Him, I encourage you to ask God to give you a revelation of how to put on this piece of spiritual armor.

Arm Yourself with Peace

So stand. . .having strapped on your feet the gospel of peace in preparation [to face the enemy with firm-footed stability and the readiness produced by the good news].

EPHESIANS 6:14–15 AMP

The peace of God arms us in a defensive and offensive manner. When we're at peace, trusting in God to take care of us, the enemy can't access our heart. When we take that peace to others by sharing the Gospel, we push back the enemy on this earth. So today, be at peace, and take His peace to others.

Arm Yourself with Faith

Above all, lift up the [protective] shield of faith
with which you can extinguish all
the flaming arrows of the evil one.

EPHESIANS 6:16 AMP

Faith is believing in something you can't see. When you're facing difficulty, remember this truth: you may not always see God's hand move or receive the answer you expect in the timing you want, but that doesn't change the fact that He is on the move and His answer is coming.

Remember, if you could see it, you wouldn't need faith. Most importantly, when you have faith, you please God.

Arm Yourself with God's Sword

And take. . .the sword of the Spirit,
which is the Word of God.
EPHESIANS 6:17 AMP

All of God's armor for us is defensive except one piece: the sword of the Spirit. We activate our sword every time we speak the Word of God. The sword strengthens and encourages and cuts fear away from our lives.

If you're sad, say, "The joy of the Lord is my strength!" If you're feeling weak: "I can do all things through Christ who strengthens me." Try using your sword today!

Arm Yourself with Prayer

With all prayer and petition pray [with specific requests] at all times [on every occasion and in every season] in the Spirit.

EPHESIANS 6:18 AMP

Recently, I saw someone act in a way I didn't think was right. It wasn't abuse or even wrong; it just didn't seem best to me. My family reminded me later that my best response is to pray. God is gently nudging all of us to come closer to Him. When we pray, we actively take a patient stance and allow God to do the moving in other people's lives.

Arm Yourself with Faith

But for right now, until that completeness,
we have three things to do to lead us toward
that consummation: Trust steadily in God,
hope unswervingly, love extravagantly.

1 CORINTHIANS 13:13 MSG

Faith is so foundational to our Christianity that Paul listed it both as a piece of God's armor and, at the end of 1 Corinthians 13, as one of the three things we hold on to as we wait for heaven.

Never lose sight of the truth that your faith will change your life.

Arm Yourself with Hope

*And now there remain: faith. . .hope [confident
expectation of eternal salvation].*
1 Corinthians 13:13 amp

The idea of heaven has always provided hope
for my future, but it has been magnified since my
brother passed away. The hope of heaven keeps
my feet moving and my heart at peace.

Whether you have loved ones there or are
simply waiting for the day Jesus will take us home,
let that hope of heaven fuel your future.

Arm Yourself with Love

*And now there remain. . .love [unselfish love for
others growing out of God's love for me],
these three [the choicest graces];
but the greatest of these is love.*

1 Corinthians 13:13 amp

God is love. Because He is in our lives, we have
more than enough ability to love others. It often
takes a conscious effort to embrace loving others,
particularly when their actions are frustrating, but
one of the best ways you can protect yourself on
this earth is by letting God's unconditional love
permeate through you to others.

RELATIONSHIPS

Recognize Your Family Is Special

[Jesus] returned to Nazareth, his hometown. . . .
Then they scoffed, "He's just the carpenter's son,
and we know Mary, his mother, and his brothers
. . . . Where did he learn all these things?"
MATTHEW 13:54–56 NLT

The people closest to you may surprise you the most, so never let your familiarity with them let you expect less of them. If they have a tug to move in an unexpected direction, encourage them to follow God's direction. You never know what big things God has planned for those around you.

Recognize Beauty

The right word at the right time is like a custom-made piece of jewelry.
PROVERBS 25:11 MSG

Our words impact others. Specifically, when we give compliments, we can greatly impact other people's lives. In fact, I still remember compliments from one, two, three, or more years ago—compliments that I am sure the person who gave them doesn't remember even saying.

So remember that your words are important. When you see someone who has done a good thing or is wearing a cute outfit, let her know. You could impact her forever.

Recognize Reprimands

And a wise friend's timely reprimand is like a gold ring slipped on your finger.
PROVERBS 25:12 MSG

No one likes to be reprimanded—but sometimes that is exactly what we need. It takes guts to speak up and suggest a change or gently berate someone, but if we never spoke up in this way, we would never have the opportunity to improve our lives.

By the way, if you are the one giving a reprimand, always remember what Paul said in Ephesians 4:15—speak the truth in love.

Recognize God's Kingdom

The kingdom of heaven is like unto a merchant man,
seeking goodly pearls: who, when he had found one
pearl of great price, went and sold all that
he had, and bought it.
MATTHEW 13:45–46 KJV

God wants us to hunt for a pearl of great price—
that piece of the kingdom of heaven—inside
each of us. That means we shouldn't dismiss
people as common or ordinary; we'll miss out on
what God can do through them. Look for God's
light in each of them—and encourage them to
let that light shine!

Recognize Sacrifice

"Yes, I know," Boaz replied. "But I also know about everything you have done for your mother-in-law since the death of your husband. . . . May the LORD, the God of Israel, under whose wings you have come to take refuge, reward you fully for what you have done."

RUTH 2:11–12 NLT

Women are great multitaskers, but that doesn't mean we should deal with the difficulty and sacrifice many endure alone. Any time you have an opportunity to help someone else out—or receive help from someone—take it! Let's bond together and invest in one another!

Recognize the Value of Wisdom

Walk with the wise and become wise;
associate with fools and get in trouble.
PROVERBS 13:20 NLT

My husband recently started going to a men's group that has many guys much older than him. It's turning out to be a huge blessing because he's learning so much from these men who have been Christians for longer than we have been on this earth.

When we choose to connect with those wiser than us—and truly listen to and heed their wisdom—we benefit greatly.

Recognize the Gift of Time

*Let each of you look not only to his
own interests, but also to the
interests of others.*

PHILIPPIANS 2:4 ESV

We live in a day when seemingly everyone is constantly checking their phone for important calls, answering e-mails, or posting photos of their latest and greatest adventures. Although our productivity is theoretically going up, the value placed on our face-to-face relationships is being tested. That's why we must realize that one of the most valuable things we can give to others is our undivided attention.

Recognize the Risks

God is there, ready to help;
I'm fearless no matter what.
Who or what can get to me?

HEBREWS 13:6 MSG

Every God-given relationship carries a certain amount of risk simply because we are human. We will make mistakes and need to forgive one another in the process. What we need to know, though, is that relationships are worth the risk. People are placed in our lives for a reason. Whether their time with you is long or short, it's well worth investing your time and energy to enjoy the journey with them.

Recognize When
Right Doesn't Matter

*It's God we are answerable to. . .not each other.
That's why Jesus lived and died and then lived again:
so that he could be our Master across the entire
range of life and death, and free us from the
petty tyrannies of each other.*
ROMANS 14:8–9 MSG

Being right boosts our pride, but it never encourages the person who is wrong. Sometimes our best interests are served when we realize the question "Who's right?" doesn't need to be answered. We're on the same team.

Recognize Unending Mercy

The steadfast love of the L<small>ORD</small> never ceases;
his mercies never come to an end;
they are new every morning;
great is your faithfulness.
L<small>AMENTATIONS</small> 3:22–23 <small>ESV</small>

Between now and when you go to sleep at night, you can use up every single one of the Lord's mercies to help you through today. The reason? Tomorrow His mercy is restocked. His mercy, grace, and love do not run out.

And because of these gifts from above, we can turn around and supply that same unending mercy in our relationships.

Recognize Their Battle Is Valid

Don't jump all over [fellow believers]
every time they do or say something
you don't agree with. . . . Remember,
they have their own history to deal
with. Treat them gently.

ROMANS 14:1 MSG

When someone is battling something I've already conquered, I need to remember what Paul writes later in Romans 14: "If there are corrections to be made or manners to be learned, God can handle that without your help."

Although our battles look different, we are fighting the same war against the enemy—and we all have been given the same victory in Jesus!

FRUITS OF THE SPIRIT

First Comes Love

But the Holy Spirit produces this kind of fruit in our lives: love, joy, peace, patience, kindness, goodness, faithfulness, gentleness, and self-control. There is no law against these things!
GALATIANS 5:22–23 NLT

God is love. He is endless. Because of this, it only makes sense that the first fruit we see in our lives as a result of living with God on our side is love. Not only is this a love for others, but it's also an understanding of God's immense love for us!

Then Comes Joy

*"Don't be dejected and sad, for the joy
of the Lord is your strength!"*

NEHEMIAH 8:10 NLT

When you know how much God loves you, you are filled with unexplainable joy. You know that, come good or bad, God will take care of you. That joy creates a unique strength in you that can only be described as supernatural.

If you need an increase of your joy today, attempt to comprehend God's love for you. Think about how much He likes being with you (He does!), and watch your joy increase as a result!

Then Comes Peace

You will keep in perfect peace all who trust in you,
all whose thoughts are fixed on you!

Isaiah 26:3 NLT

On a recent trip to my in-laws, my one-year-old was sleeping on the floor in the guest room. In the morning, I pulled him onto my tummy, and we laid there for another twenty minutes. He wasn't sleeping; neither was I. We were just resting. He knew he was safe in my arms.

God's unfathomable peace can be yours; find yourself a place where you can simply rest in His presence. There, you'll find peace.

Then Comes Patience

But what happens when we live God's way? . . .
We develop a willingness to stick with things.
GALATIANS 5:22–23 MSG

When I'm at church or out with my boys, I'm often tempted to check my phone. Every time I do, though, I'm letting impatience rule me. I'm not focusing on and enjoying the moment I'm in.

When we let God's Spirit reside in us, we continue to strengthen our patience muscle. We learn to stick with listening, forgiveness, and grace. We can focus on the moment because we know God is at work.

Then Comes Gentleness

*We develop. . .a sense
of compassion in the heart.*
GALATIANS 5:22–23 MSG

At this point, God can begin to turn our focus outward. The Spirit has settled His love in our hearts, which brings us joy and peace. He's started to work on our patience in dealing with what life brings us. Now, we can look at others differently. We know God loves them dearly, and as a result, we become more compassionate.

Get used to this nudging to be gentle in action and attitude toward others. It's the Spirit at work in your heart.

Then Comes Goodness

We develop. . .a conviction that a basic holiness
permeates things and people.
GALATIANS 5:22–23 MSG

After the Spirit stirs in us a sense of compassion, that gentleness begins to see goodness in other people. We start to focus on people's strengths, not their weaknesses.

Your natural tendency may be to focus on negative things, so don't be alarmed when you sense this tug toward goodness as the Spirit grows in you. Instead, let your thoughts turn in that direction. It's God's goodness coming to you so it can flow through you to others.

Then Comes Faithfulness

We find ourselves involved in
loyal commitments.
GALATIANS 5:22–23 MSG

Once we've developed a sense of wholeness in our personal life and have started to bring that wholeness to our relationships, the Spirit of God works on our commitment level. No longer are we patient one day and a brat the next; we're not a roller coaster of emotions or temperamental as we deal with people. A can-do attitude develops on the inside that says, *I commit to living this way!* We begin to mirror God's faithfulness in our schedule, personal life, and relationships.

Then Comes Meekness

We find ourselves. . .not needing
to force our way in life.
GALATIANS 5:22–23 MSG

As the Spirit continues to increase your faithfulness, you start to realize that forcefulness is not a virtue. Meekness is. Some people associate meekness with weakness or backing down, but the opposite is actually true. Meekness provides the strength you need to stand in the position God has placed you. Humility allows you to confidently pursue God's purpose, knowing God will open the opportunities you need to make that happen. Without Him, you can do nothing; with Him, you can do all things.

Then Comes Self-Control

*We find ourselves. . .able to marshal
and direct our energies wisely.*
GALATIANS 5:22–23 MSG

Self-control is one of the hardest disciplines of life
to stay consistent in. It's good to know that as we
grow in the Spirit, He helps us control our selfish
desires. That means He helps us say no to that
extra piece of chocolate and say yes to exercise.
He helps us hold our temper and stay focused at
work. He helps us put Him first and us second!

All by His Spirit

But what happens when we live God's way?
He brings gifts into our lives, much the same
way that fruit appears in an orchard.

GALATIANS 5:22 MSG

Have you ever seen an apple tree straining to grow apples? Trees don't have to work hard to create fruit. As long as they stay connected to their roots, fruit will appear.

In the same way, when we stay connected to the Holy Spirit, we abide in the vine of our heavenly Father and we will bear the fruit of the Spirit we read about in Galatians chapter 5!

OUR FUTURE

The Need for Wisdom Is Coming

Some things Paul writes are difficult to understand.
Irresponsible people who don't know what they
are talking about twist them every which way.
2 PETER 3:16 MSG

We're living in a time when people come up with both convincing and crazy reasons why the Bible isn't real. We need wisdom from God to know how to sense what is truth, what isn't, and how to respond to both. If you're in that situation right now, pray for God's wisdom. He will respond!

Difficulty Is Coming

*You did it: you changed wild lament into whirling
dance; you ripped off my black mourning band
and decked me with wildflowers.*

PSALM 30:11 MSG

Life can be intimidating. A bad doctor's report
or financial difficulty can turn your world upside
down. But just as quickly as negative circumstances come into our lives, we can always remind
ourselves that anything can happen. God can turn
our lives around in moments.

Keep focused on Him; He will bring you
through.

Our Permanent Home Is Coming

So we don't look at the troubles we can see now;
rather, we fix our gaze on things that cannot be
seen. For the things we see now will soon be gone,
but the things we cannot see will last forever.

2 CORINTHIANS 4:18 NLT

My grandpa Carl lived for three years longer than his wife of sixty-three years. During that time, I watched him embody the truth that earth is temporary. He knew he would soon meet with his wife in heaven and bow together before our Lord.

May we live knowing heaven is near.

Tribulation Is Coming

*"So when all these things begin
to happen, stand and look up,
for your salvation is near!"*
Luke 21:28 NLT

Terrorism, bullies, criminals, natural disasters—this world is filled with negative circumstances that can overwhelm our lives with fear and worry. When that happens to me, I walk outside and look up. I stare at the sky, clouds, and sun. The Creator of those natural things created my heart and my life. He knows exactly what is going on in this world—and He knows how to keep you and me safe.

Endless Light Is Coming

And there will be no night there—no
need for lamps or sun—for the Lord
God will shine on them. And they
will reign forever and ever.

REVELATION 22:5 NLT

I hate evil. It runs rampant in the world and messes up so many people's lives. I often look forward to the day when darkness will be defeated and light alone will rule and reign on this earth. Keeping my focus there makes these moments much more bearable.

Jesus Is Coming

For the Lord himself shall descend from heaven with a shout, with the voice of the archangel, and with the trump of God: and the dead in Christ shall rise first: then we which are alive and remain shall be caught up together with them in the clouds, to meet the Lord in the air: and so shall we ever be with the Lord.
1 Thessalonians 4:16–17 KJV

Jesus will soon be coming to earth to bring everyone who believes in Him as Savior to heaven, our eternal home. How glorious that will be!

Endless Provision Is Coming

On each side of the river grew a tree
of life, bearing twelve crops of fruit,
with a fresh crop each month.
The leaves were used for medicine
to heal the nations.

<small>REVELATION 22:2 NLT</small>

Every once in a while, it's good to remember how lavish God has created heaven. Gold streets, mansions, trees producing new fruit every month—think of what our future includes! If He will provide for our future so extravagantly, trust Him to provide for you here on this earth as well.

The Finish Line Is Coming

"But I do not account my life of any value nor as precious to myself, if only I may finish my course and the ministry that I received from the Lord Jesus, to testify to the gospel of the grace of God."

ACTS 20:24 ESV

I have many good memories growing up in church, loving Jesus, and serving in ministry. But none of that matters if I don't finish my race as an adult. God wants us to serve Him in the beginning and the end. Run with the finish line in mind.

Justice Is Coming

*And the devil who had deceived them was thrown
into the lake of fire and sulfur where the beast and
the false prophet were, and they will be tormented
day and night forever and ever.*

REVELATION 20:10 ESV

When the enemy seems to overrun your life, back
yourself up from the situation. Remind yourself
that his time of justice will come. He will receive
his eternal reward. In the end, God wins. Stay on
His side and you will win too.

Your Reward Is Coming

Each one's work will become manifest, for the Day
will disclose it, because it will be revealed by fire,
and the fire will test what sort of work each one
has done. If the work that anyone has built on the
foundation survives, he will receive a reward.

1 Corinthians 3:13–14 ESV

It's easy to crave attention from others. If we seek that attention alone, though, we'll forget our main audience is in heaven. When God is pleased, it doesn't matter who notices. We will eventually receive a reward from Him.

A Beautiful Home Is Coming

And the twelve gates were twelve pearls, each of the gates made of a single pearl, and the street of the city was pure gold, like transparent glass.

REVELATION 21:21 ESV

Everything God does exudes beauty. The beauty you see here on earth is only a fraction of the beauty we will see one day in heaven. Keeping our eyes on what awaits us in heaven will keep this life on earth in perspective. Because God loves us, we have a beautiful home waiting for us on the other side of this life.